Across the Big Blue Sea

AN OCEAN WILDLIFE BOOK

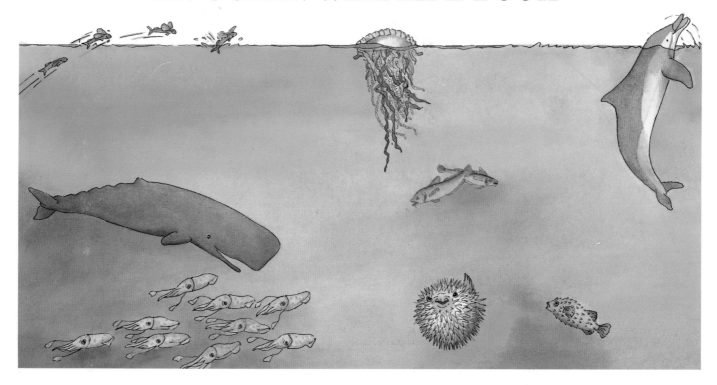

Jakki Wood

■ NATIONAL GEOGRAPHIC SOCIETY

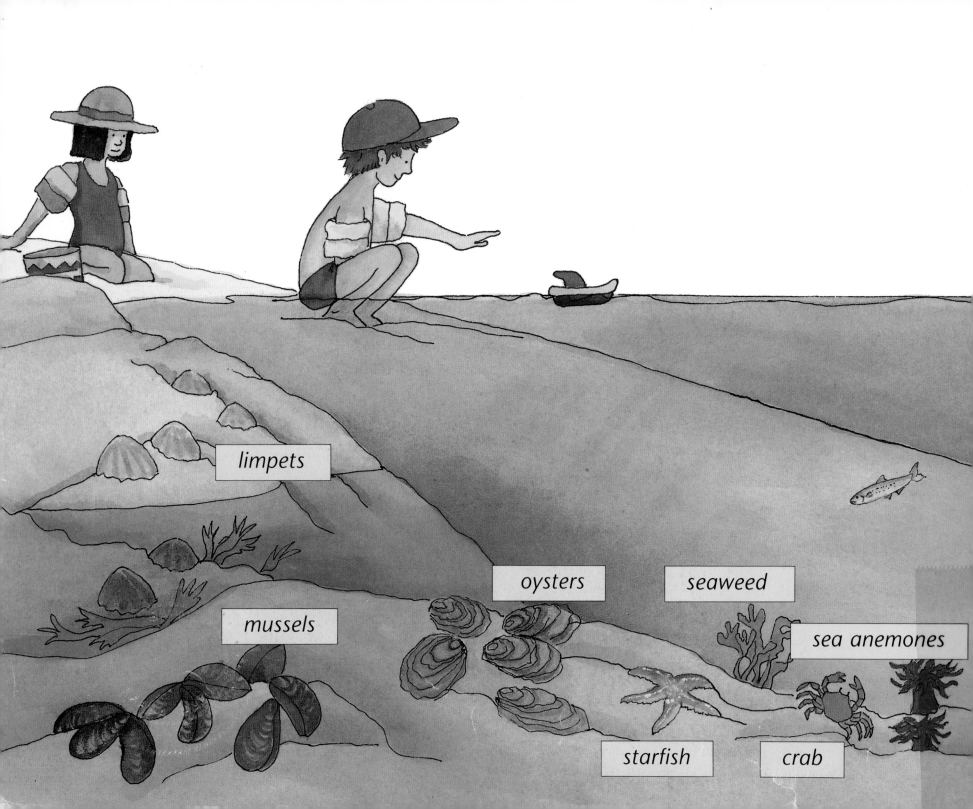

limpets

mussels

oysters

seaweed

sea anemones

starfish

crab

On a beach in California, Tom gives his boat a *push!*

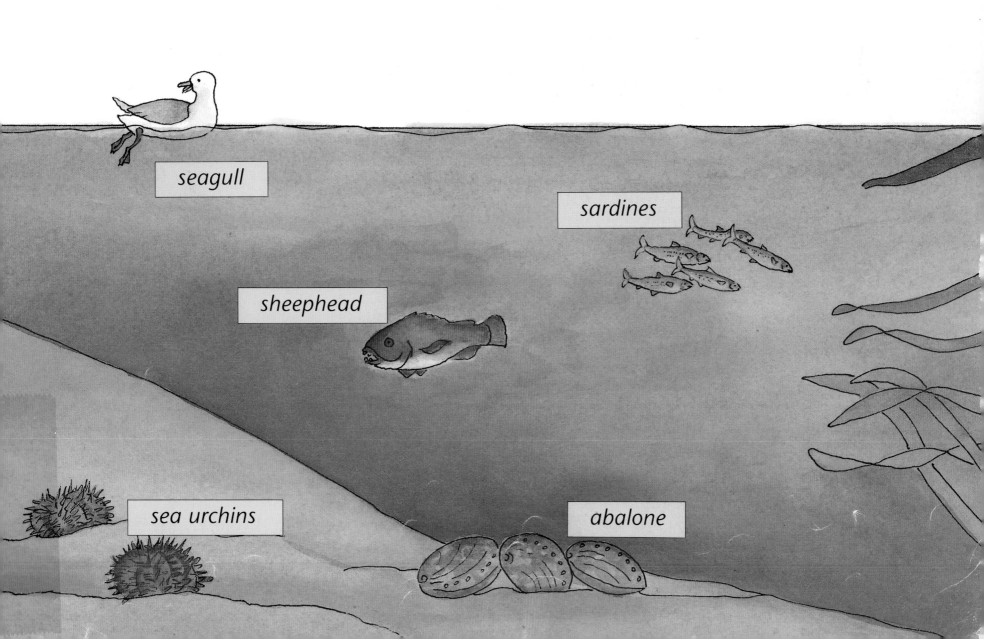

seagull

sardines

sheephead

sea urchins

abalone

"Have a nice trip," he calls, as the boat drifts away on the ocean currents.

brown pelican

anchovies

Out in the Pacific, killer whales play with Tom's boat ...

tuna

but they don't stop it.

Pacific salmon

killer whale

thresher shark

Splash! Flying fish leap and glide.

flying fish

gray whale

octopus

black smoker

Tom's boat is just north of Australia,
near a tiny coral island.

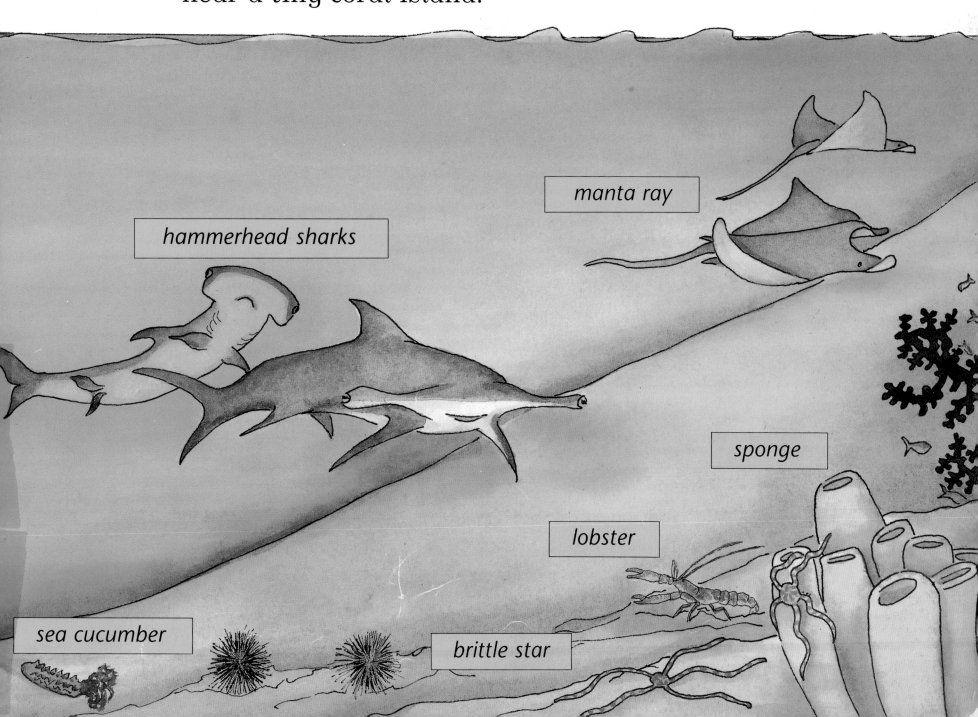

manta ray

hammerhead sharks

sponge

lobster

sea cucumber

brittle star

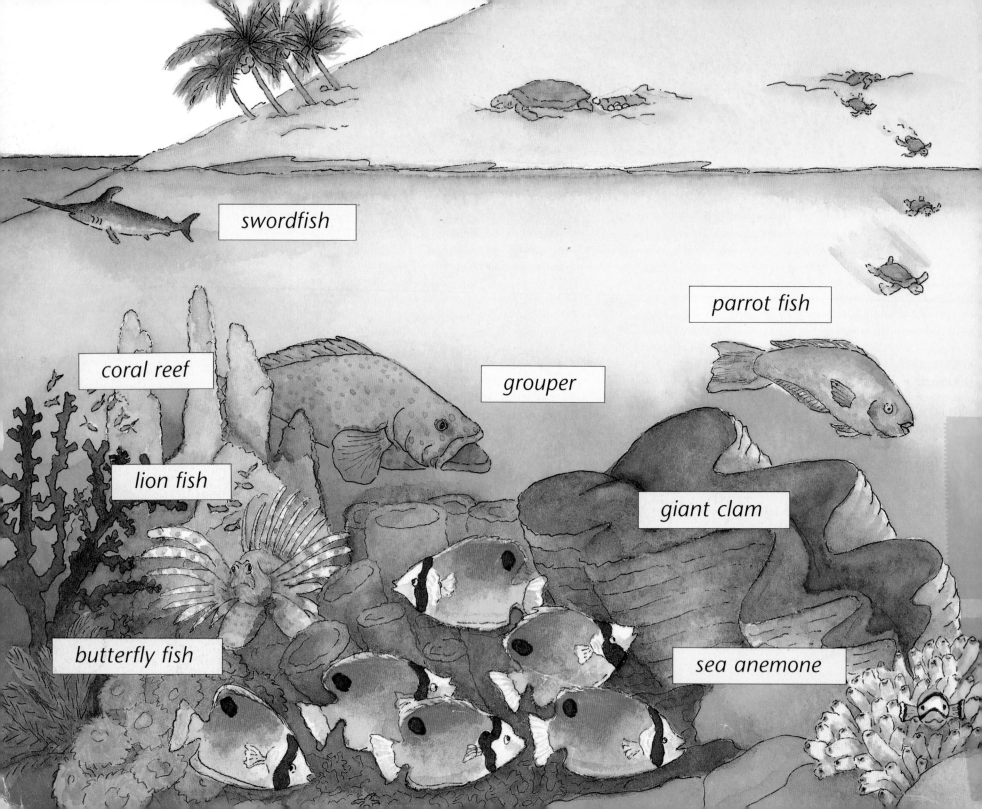

swordfish

parrot fish

coral reef

grouper

lion fish

giant clam

butterfly fish

sea anemone

A friendly turtle gives the boat a ride.

clownfish

trunkfish

loggerhead turtle

In the Indian Ocean, a great storm blows up.

Fish swim calmly beneath the waves.

scad

whalebird

macaroni penguin

Safe from the storm, south of Africa,
the boat is noticed by some curious penguins ...

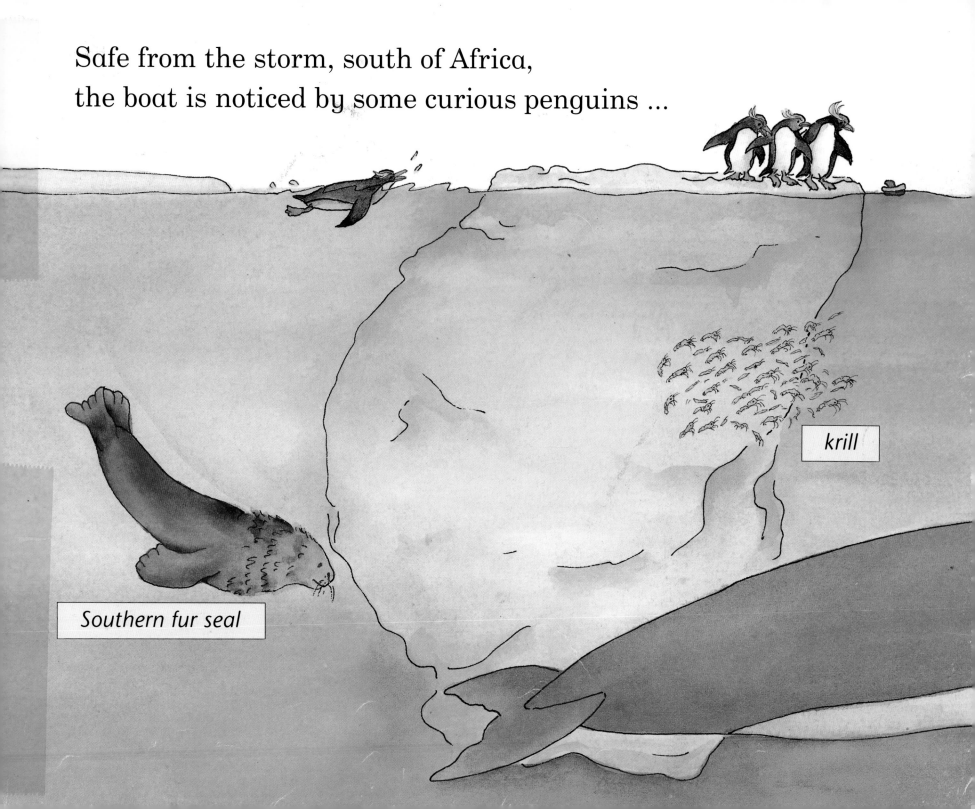

krill

Southern fur seal

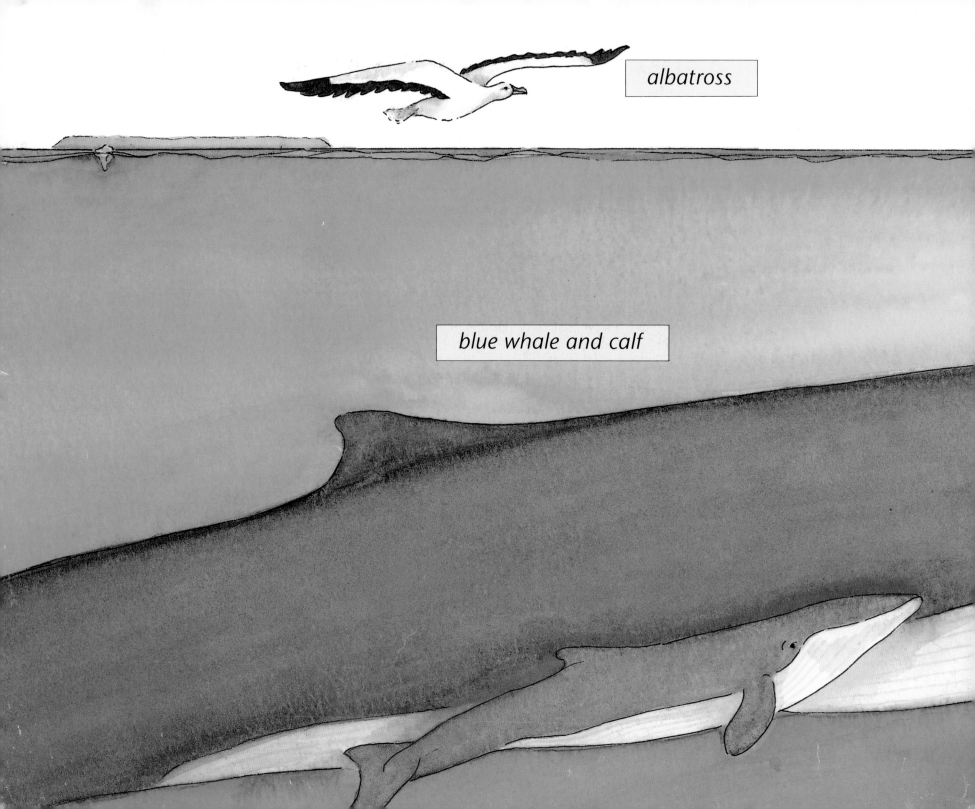

albatross

blue whale and calf

and watched by a huge blue whale.

Tom's boat has reached the Atlantic Ocean.

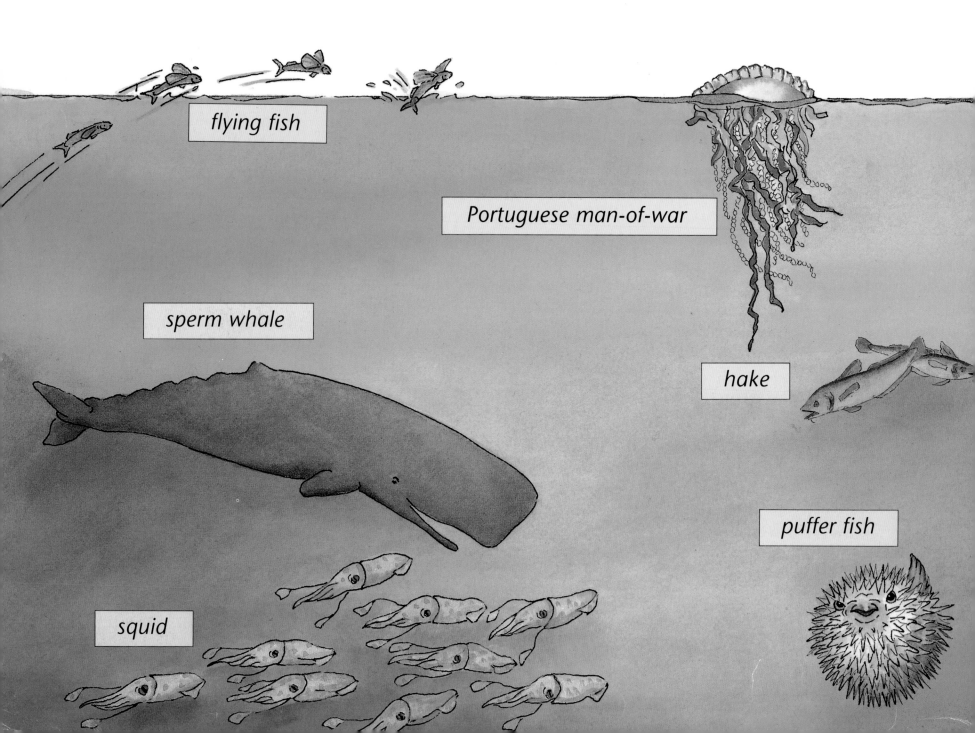

flying fish

Portuguese man-of-war

sperm whale

hake

puffer fish

squid

The dolphins would like to play with it.

common dolphin

But the warm current carries it above the wreck of a pirate ship ...

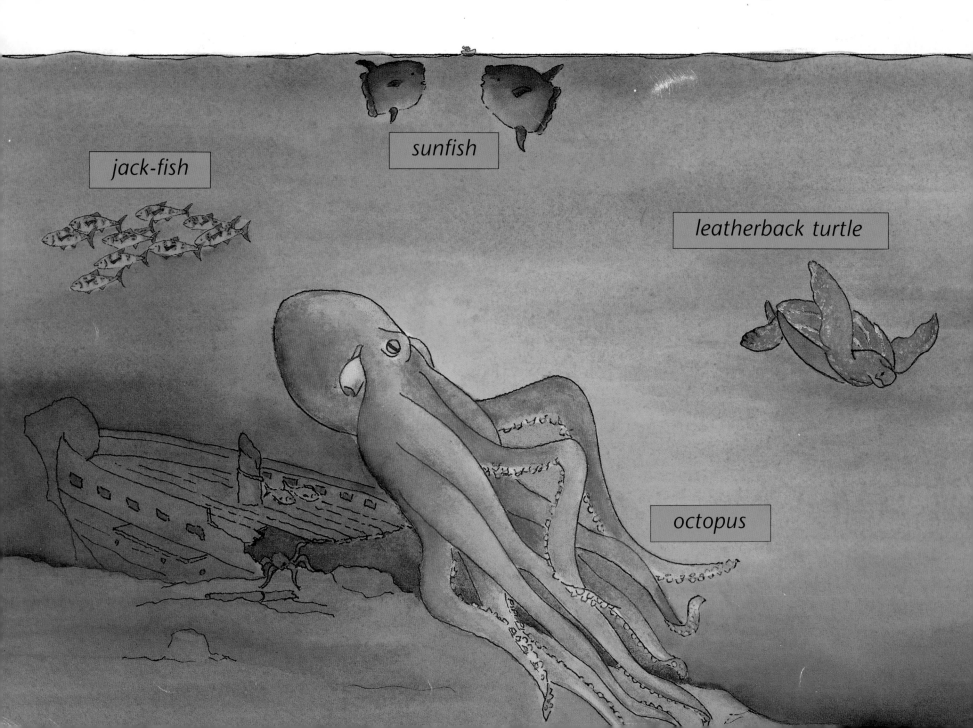

through the Sargasso Sea ...

sailfish

sargassum weed

eel

and right across the Atlantic Ocean.

porbeagle shark

hatchet fish

angler fish

gulper eel

Far, far below, strange creatures swim in the dark water.

squid

black smoker

At last Tom's boat is close to land again.

cormorant

herring

A dolphin pushes the boat towards the shore.

bottlenose dolphin

pilot whale

seagull

puffin

stingray

cod

gray seal

John Dory

Tom's boat has drifted to the coast of Great Britain.
And a boy there wants to play!

mackerel

plaice

cockles

crab

Can you follow the little boat's journey? The blue line shows the route it takes, drifting with the wind and the ocean currents.

Look at some of the fish and other sea creatures on the map. They will help you to match areas of the map to the story inside. Follow the arrows from California on the western coast of the United States to the southwestern coast of Great Britain—a sea journey of almost 25,000 miles.

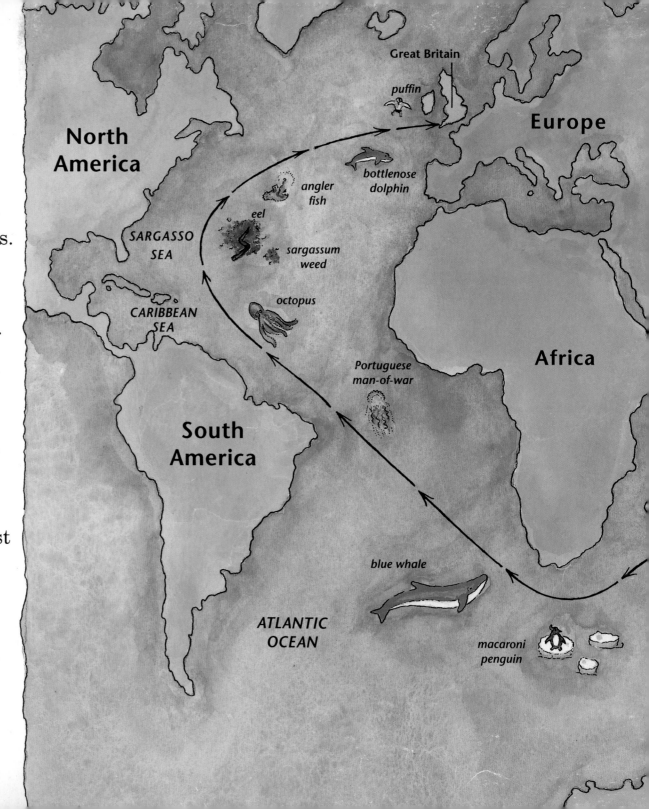